The Camel Fair

Written by Wendy Cooling

Contents

Delhi

Dear Lee,

I'm on holiday in India, visiting Dad's family, and it's really exciting. I hope you got my postcard of the Red Fort from Delhi.

The Old Delhi streets are really busy.

Delhi is two cities in one, New and Old Delhi. Old Delhi is amazing, with people, animals and **bazaars** all crammed into the narrow streets. New Delhi has lots of big buildings and open spaces.

We stayed in New Delhi with Dad's family for a week, but then we travelled to Pushkar – that's in Rajasthan – to see the Camel Fair.

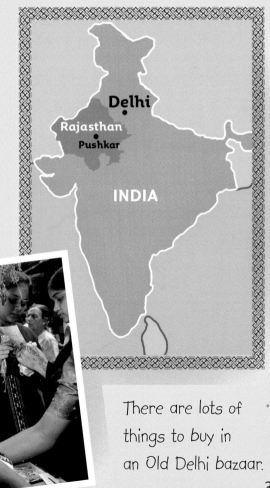

There are lots of things to buy in an Old Delhi bazaar.

3

Journey to Pushkar

The Pushkar Camel Fair is very famous. People come long distances to buy and sell camels, but they also come to enjoy themselves.

In Rajasthan camels are very important, especially for people who live in the desert and in villages. People use camels to get themselves and their things from place to place, they drink camel milk and camel hair is used to make rugs, tents and clothing. Even camel **dung** is collected, dried and sold as fuel for cooking fires.

5

To get to Pushkar, we had to drive along a huge main
road. I couldn't believe it when we saw camel carts
coming along towards us on the wrong side of the road!
This was so that they could turn off into villages rather
than drive to the next exit. It was
quite scary at first.

Then we saw the tiny town of Pushkar, right on the edge
of the Thar Desert.

The Thar Desert

- This desert is also called the Great Indian Desert.

- It is HUGE – about 800 kilometres long and
  480 kilometres
  wide. The biggest
  part is in Rajasthan.

- It has rolling sand
  dunes that look like
  yellow snowdrifts.

- It has lots of small
  bushes and trees
  with leaves that grow almost to the ground, so camels can
  graze on them.

- Many people live in the desert. Some live in tiny villages
  with cool mud huts, others in larger villages with hot brick
  houses. Nomads travel from place to place.

- The people grow crops using water from wells and from
  a canal.

Pushkar, the holy place

Pushkar is a holy place for Hindus. They say that Lord Brahma dropped a lotus flower from the sky into the desert. Water appeared as if by magic and a beautiful lake was formed. Temples were built around the lake and then the little town of Pushkar grew up.

Hindus come from all over to make **Puja** here. It's a religious blessing. In Pushkar, when you make Puja, you drop rose petals into the water. When you've done your Puja the priest ties an orange thread around your wrist. You're supposed to keep this on until it wears out and falls off.

जगत पिताश्री ब्रह्मा मंदिर.

These people are waiting to enter a temple.

Desert Camp

The Camel Fair is held on the sand dunes just outside the little town of Pushkar. It lasts for ten days and about 200,000 people visit. There isn't room for everyone to stay in the town, so we stayed in a city of tents called "Desert Camp".

There were rows and rows of orange and white striped tents. Some of them were big enough for 60 people to sleep in! Our tent was only for four people. It was cosy, but the beds were just boards and were very hard!

At the Camel Fair

Each day at the Camel Fair there are camel auctions, where traders buy and sell camels. There are camel shows and camel races, too.

All the camels are decorated and look quite amazing. They wear necklaces of tinsel and flowers, and some of them are painted with beautiful patterns in henna. There are rows and rows of stalls nearby selling bells, ribbons and other decorations just for the camels!

12

Camel facts

- Camels are very strong mammals with wide, padded feet. They have bushy eyebrows and long eyelashes to protect their eyes from desert sand.

- A camel with one hump is called a dromedary, or Arabian camel.

- A camel with two humps is called a Bactrian camel.

- The wild Bactrian camel is an **endangered species**.

- A camel's hump contains fat, not water, and the camel can go without food and water for three or four days.

a fat-filled hump

long eyelashes and bushy eyebrows

An Arabian camel

two-toed feet with leathery pads

large nostrils that can open and close

a long tail

thick, shaggy fur

A Bactrian camel

All the colours of the fair

All around, there are women and girls in saris of the brightest colours you've ever seen. Some wear swinging, bright **ghaghara** skirts and tie-dyed blouses glittering with silver tinsel and silver jewellery. Many men and boys wear bright turbans and dress in white.

There are pilgrims dressed in orange with bowls and walking sticks, villagers, tribal people from the desert and masses of tourists. Some of the pilgrims have walked for months across India to get here for the festival and the fair.

Camel racing

The camels at the fair are usually work animals. But at the camel races, they are treated like race horses – their owners decorate and groom them, and then they race!

It's very noisy with the crowds shouting at the camels they want to win, and the riders shouting at their camels to go faster.

There aren't any **stirrups** and the riders have to be very careful not to fall off. Some of them wrap one leg around their camel's neck to help them to stay on. Camels run in a very odd, lollopy sort of a way – it's not like a gallop, just a high-speed trot!

19

Getting on a Camel

1 The camel kneels down.

2 You climb on its back, just behind the hump.

6 The camel sways as it walks – it's quite nice when you get used to it.

5 Don't get dizzy! When the camel is standing up, you are a long way from the ground.

3 The camel gets up
   and jerks its head
   and long neck forward.

4 You must hold on very
   tight otherwise you'll
   shoot over its head.

Camel moods

Camels aren't the bad-tempered creatures that people say they are. Sometimes they kick and spit, but they are also very patient and intelligent.
They grunt and bawl when they have to stand up carrying something heavy, just like a weightlifter does in a competition.

Grr ...
this is heavy.

Food and drink

At the Camel Fair there are stalls everywhere selling bracelets, clothes, **souvenirs**, bags and of course food! Meat is forbidden in this holy place (even eggs aren't allowed because they might hatch), so all the delicious things on the stalls are made from vegetables, grains or fruit.

Everyone drinks chai, a kind of very sweet tea. It's made by boiling heavily spiced tea in water with sweetened milk. The **nomadic** camel traders from the desert like to **bargain** over a cup of chai.

The camels have to eat and drink as well.
There are heaps of camel feed for them on the edge of the fairground.

My favourite Pushkar menu

Breakfast
Dal and chapattis
(lentils with pancakes)
A cup of chai

Lunch
Samosas (little pastry triangles
filled with vegetables)
Pakora (potato and spinach cakes)
Lassi (a yogurt drink)

Dinner
Vegetable thali (small tastes of different
food – I liked the **dosas** and **sabzi** best)
A mango (a sweet and juicy orange
coloured fruit)

Sunset at Pushkar

At sunset there are campfires everywhere. The sounds of temple bells and drums drift across from the town and there's music of all kinds. The camels look wonderful as the sun sets. The Ferris wheels and roundabouts start. There's open-air theatre and dancing and no one wants the evening to end ...

Down by the lake, when it gets dark, people float tiny clay lamps on leaf boats so that the water is lit up by these bobbing lights. It's magical. The town is a mass of lights and colours at night and the streets are full of people eating and having fun.

The last day

It's my last day and I've seen some baby camels –
they are so sweet.

Baby camels

Baby camels are often born white.

Baby males are called bull calves.

Baby females are called heifers.

Now we must drive back to Delhi and I'm making a wish
to come back. I won't forget the Pushkar Camel Fair, ever!

Love from your best friend,

Sarina

Glossary

auctions	when something is sold to the person who offers the most money
bargain	to buy something for the best price
bazaars	streets of small stalls
dosas	pancakes made from lentil flour
dung	manure, or animal droppings
endangered species	a type of animal at serious risk of becoming extinct
ghaghara	a flowing skirt worn by Rajasthani women
henna	a reddish dye made from powdered leaves of the henna plant
nomadic	moving from place to place to find food and water
Puja	a Hindu blessing
sabzi	curried vegetables
souvenirs	gifts that remind you of somewhere
stalls	somewhere to sell things from, like in a market
stirrups	metal loops through which riders put their feet

Index

Ideas for guided reading

Learning objectives: read examples of letters written to recount; compare the way information is presented; use phonological, contextual and grammatical knowledge to predict the meaning of unfamiliar words; work effectively in groups by ensuring each member takes a turn, challenging, supporting and moving on.

Curriculum links: Geography - Where in the World is Barnaby Bear? Passport to the World; Citizenship – Living in a Diverse World.

Interest Words: Delhi, Pushkar, Rajasthan, nomads, Hindus, Lord Brahma, lotus flower, Puja, tinsel, dromedary, pilgrims, lollopy, patient, weightlifters, forbidden, chai, chapattis, samosas.

Word count: 1,417

Getting started

This book can be read over two guided reading sessions.

- Before showing the book, ask the children if they have ever been to a fair and to describe what they found, e.g. *Ferris wheel, candyfloss.* Ask the children to suggest how the Camel Fair might be similar or different.

- Introduce the book by reading the title, blurb and contents to the children. Can they say what kind of text this is and explain how they know?

- Allow the children some time to browse through the pictures and to read chapter headings. Which parts of this book do they think will interest them the most and why?

- Read pp2–3 to the children, demonstrating how you infer the meaning of the word in bold by reading around it. Ask the children to suggest what they can do to check if their meaning is correct (check the glossary).

Reading and responding

- Ask the children to read pp4–7 silently and be prepared to share one or two interesting facts. Which facts are the easiest to find and share? Discuss the use of bullet points and their presentation in a box.

- Ask the children to read from pp8–29 silently and independently, while you